P9-CLB-810

Cornerstones of Freedom

Valley Forge

R. Conrad Stein

CHILDRENS PRESS®
CHICAGO

Library of Congress Cataloging-in-Publication Data

Stein, R. Conrad.
    Valley Forge / by R. Conrad Stein.
        p. cm. – (Cornerstones of freedom)
    ISBN 0-516-06683-8
    1. United States—History—Revolution, 1775–1783—Juvenile
literature. 2. Washington, George, 1732–1799—Headquarters
—Pennsylvania—Valley Forge—Juvenile literature. 3. Valley
Forge (Pa.)—History—Juvenile literature. 4. Valley Forge
National Historical Park (Pa.)—Juvenile literature. [1. United
States—History—Revolution, 1775–1783—Campaigns.
2. Valley Forge (Pa.)—History.] I. Title. II. Series.
E234.S833 1994
973.7– dc20   94-9490
                                                                CIP
                                                                AC

George Washington

For General George Washington and the American army, 1777 was the most frustrating year of the Revolutionary War. Earlier, Washington and his troops were driven out of New York and began a long, dismal retreat across the plains of New Jersey. The relentless British advance was so discouraging that patriot Thomas Paine was moved to write, "These are the times that try men's souls."

Late in the year, the British marched toward Philadelphia. At the time, Philadelphia served as the capital of the infant American republic. General Washington believed that the fall of the city would be a disaster for the nation. Determined to stop the British, he moved his army to a Pennsylvania stream called the Brandywine.

On September 11, 1777, a deafening roar rocked the banks of the little river as both sides exchanged cannon fire. When the smoke of the explosions cleared, waves of British soldiers swept out of the woods and splashed across the river. The red-coated troops pointed their muskets forward, and their long bayonets glistened in the sun. The river valley was swept with the ugly sounds of battle. Terrified horses neighed. Wounded and dying men screamed. The booming voices of commanders thundered out orders. Cannon blasts sounded like the devil's own drumbeats.

From atop his horse, General Washington watched and worried. He knew that the British outnumbered his men, but from what he could determine, the Redcoats seemed to be advancing with only small units. Was the main British force behind those small units? Did the British commander consider Washington's army to be so trifling a foe that he was attacking with only half his soldiers? Through noon, the awful battle

The Battle of the Brandywine

raged on. The once clear water of the Brandywine flowed red. And General Washington worried.

Suddenly, a deadly hail of musket fire burst out of the trees behind the American lines. Redcoats by the thousands swarmed down on Washington's men. The Americans were trapped between the river waters and the charging British.

In an instant, George Washington realized his mistake. The British commander, General Howe, had preoccupied the Americans by sending small bands of soldiers across the river. Meanwhile, the main body of Redcoats had curved upstream and crossed the Brandywine at an unguarded point. General Washington cursed. The British had used the same tactic a year earlier when driving the American forces out of Long Island, New York. Worse yet, Washington had stationed scouts along the upper banks of the Brandywine, but no reliable word of a British crossing had come forth. In war, ignorance of the enemy's movements is usually fatal.

The battle at Brandywine almost became a rout. Only Washington's skilled generalship prevented a disaster. He sent his best division to engage the British forces that stormed the American rear. He then led an orderly withdrawal of the main body of American troops. By nightfall, the Americans had at least escaped annihilation.

Brandywine was another depressing loss for the American army. It also served as a bitter taste of the horrors of war. An American private named Elisha Stevens summed up the daylong ordeal in these words: "The battle at Brandywine began in the morning and held till night without

Brandywine proved to be another victory for British General Howe (right) over George Washington.

6

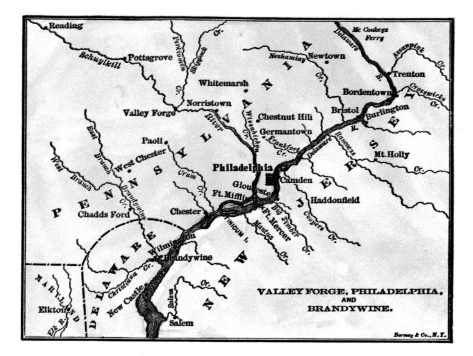

This map shows the area surrounding Philadelphia in 1777. After their victory at the Brandywine, the British were free to march northeast to Philadelphia, the American capital. Northwest of Philadelphia is Valley Forge, where General Washington chose to winter his troops.

much cessation of arms, cannon roaring, muskets cracking, drums beating, bombs flying all around; men [were] a dying, wounded [men's] horrid groans [were enough] to grieve the hardest of hearts. . . ."

The defeat left Philadelphia open to the British army. On September 26, 1777, the Redcoats marched into the American capital. It was a staggering blow to the new nation. All over the country, people spoke in hushed tones, wondering fearfully if the American soldiers would ever defeat the British.

During the early stages of the Revolutionary War, the American army suffered from two dismaying shortcomings. First, its officers had no experience fighting European troops. Previously, the Americans had fought against

The American army was made up of amateur soldiers who were poorly trained and lacked adequate supplies.

Indians. The Indian wars called for entirely different tactics than doing battle with well-drilled, well-armed Europeans. Second, the American soldiers were amateurs compared to the professionally trained British Redcoats. The Americans lacked the ability to maneuver and march in precise formation as could the British.

But the American army, despite the string of defeats it had suffered, retained remarkable spirit. Even the lowliest private had a profound belief in the rightness of his cause. While the

beaten soldiers fell back from the Brandywine
River, a captain named Enoch Anderson wrote,
"I saw not a despairing look, nor did I hear a
despairing word. We had solacing words always
ready for each other—'Come, boys, we shall do
better another time.' Had a man suggested, or
even hinted the idea of giving up, he would have
been knocked down. . . . "

The winds soon turned icy, and sleet rained
down on the Pennsylvania pine trees. With
winter approaching, the British troops made

themselves comfortable in the warm homes of Philadelphia residents. General Washington, on the other hand, faced the momentous decision of choosing winter quarters for his army of 11,000 men. Washington could move his soldiers to Reading or Lancaster. But he wanted his army camp nearer Philadelphia to discourage any further British advances. So he decided to winter his troops on a rolling plain that commanded the high ground several miles outside the city. The plain would be remembered forever in American history. It was called Valley Forge.

The march to Valley Forge was a nightmare for the exhausted soldiers. After many months

in the field, they lacked clothing, proper food, and even boots for their feet. The journey began in late December while powdery snow whistled through the ranks of the Americans. Wounded men clung to their comrades' shoulders as the long column inched over the roadway. Valley Forge lay only thirteen miles away, but it took Washington's weary troops nearly a week to hike there. Many of the soldiers, whose boots had worn out long ago,

wrapped their feet in rags. A bitter George Washington wrote, "you might have tracked the army . . . to Valley Forge by the blood on their feet."

The Americans limped onto the windswept plain called Valley Forge before Christmas, 1777. Here they found open fields and forests, but no shelter. It was the most forbidding place to spend a winter that any of them could imagine. A Connecticut soldier named James Sullivan Martin wrote, "We arrived at Valley Forge in the evening. It was dark, there was no water to be found, and I was perishing with thirst. I searched for water till I was weary. . . . I felt at that instant as if I would have taken [food] or drink from the best friend I had on

When they arrived at Valley Forge, the troops had to sleep in the open, exposed to the frigid air.

earth by force. I am not writing fiction, all are sober realities."

On the evening of December 23, General Washington sat in a drafty tent, surrounded by shivering officers, and wrote a long, pleading letter to the leaders of the American Congress. "What is to become of the Army this winter?" he asked. "We have . . . no less than 2,898 men now in camp [who] are barefoot and otherwise naked." The general then complained about Congressmen who dwell "in a comfortable room by a good fireside" while the common soldier "occupies a cold, bleak hill and sleeps under frost and snow without clothes or blankets."

Washington's letter cut to the heart of the supply problems plaguing the American army. In order to win battles, the men needed ammunition, horses, clothing, proper food, and medical supplies. But the young American republic lacked the organization to deliver these items on a regular basis. Government officials could not decide if the war should be financed by the individual states or by the national government.

There was also the problem of profiteers. These were American businessmen who claimed to be patriots, but who reaped enormous profits by selling goods to the army at outrageous prices. About these businessmen, Washington wrote: "I would to God that one of the most atrocious [of the profiteers] of each state was hung upon a gallows. . . . No punishment in my

A modern re-creation of George Washington's headquarters tent at Valley Forge, which provided him little protection from the snow and bone-chilling wind

opinion is too great for the man who can build his greatness upon his country's ruin."

Because of the chaotic government and unchecked profiteering, the troops shivered with fever and ached with hunger at Valley Forge. Many officers feared that the men, despite their marvelous spirit, would give up in disgust and walk home. Washington warned Congress that unless he was given proper supplies, his army "must inevitably be reduced to one of these three things: starve, dissolve, or disperse."

There was still work to do in the winter camp. Washington ordered the troops to cut down trees both for firewood and the construction of huts. Thomas Paine, who visited the camp as the building got underway, described the scene: it was "like a family of beavers, everyone busy; some carrying logs, others mud, and the rest fastening them

Soldiers building huts at Valley Forge

together." Street by street and hut by hut, a surprisingly neat little city rose on the snow-swept fields. George Washington remained in his drafty tent until many of his men were housed in the log huts. Washington then moved into a stone house owned by a local man named Isaac Potts.

During the building of the cabins, the men suffered from near-starvation rations. While they worked, they often chanted, "No bread, no meat. No bread, no meat!" One soldier complained that his "holiday meal" consisted of nothing more than rice and a few teaspoons of vinegar.

None of the troops had proper clothing. Their coats, trousers, and boots had worn to shreds during the summer campaigns. One soldier on guard duty was seen standing on his hat to keep his bare feet out of the snow. A regimental doctor named Albigence Waldo gave this description of a typical enlisted man suffering through this terrible winter:

Reconstructed soldiers' huts stand today at Valley Forge. Inside the huts, the conditions were cramped and primitive.

There comes a soldier; his bare feet are seen through his worn-out shoes, his legs nearly naked from the tattered remains of an only pair of stockings, his breeches not sufficient to cover his nakedness, his shirt hanging in strings. . . . He comes and cries with an air of wretchedness and despair, 'I am sick, my feet lame, my legs are sore, my body covered with this tormenting itch.'

Dreadful diseases such as typhus, smallpox, and pneumonia swept the camp. Before the winter ended, the casualties from disease and malnutrition numbered in the hundreds. The dead were buried in unmarked graves at Valley Forge.

In the midst of January 1778, when Washington's army was at its lowest ebb, American General James Mitchell Varnum wrote this despairing letter: "The situation of the camp [at Valley Forge] is such that in all human probability the army must soon dissolve. Many of the troops are destitute. . . . The horses are dying for want of forage. The country in the vicinity of the camp is exhausted. What consequences have we rationally to expect? Our desertions are . . . great. The love of freedom, which once animated the breasts of those born in the country, is controlled by hunger, the keenest of necessities."

Facing these outrageous conditions, many other armies would have either risen up in mutiny or deserted as a group. And, indeed, many desperate young men did flee their miserable winter quarters. Still, there was no widespread unrest among the troops. Also, for every one deserter, a hundred more stayed to fight again in the spring. Writing from a snowbound log cabin, Colonel John Brooks of Massachusetts claimed: "In my opinion nothing but virtue has kept our army together through this [winter]. There has been the great principle, the love of our country, which first called us to the field, and that only, to influence us."

A trickle of supplies began rolling into the camp with the appointment of a new quartermaster general. In early 1778, Congress asked Nathanael Greene to tackle the rugged job of supplying the American army. Greene was a loyal officer who wanted to remain with the men of his division, but he accepted the job of

Nathanael Greene, quartermaster of the American army

quartermaster because he recognized its importance. General Greene was no miracle worker. He could not produce supplies where none existed. Yet he rummaged diligently through government storehouses and sent every blanket, coat, and pair of boots he could find to the freezing men at Valley Forge. About the winter camp, Greene later told Washington, "God grant we may never be brought to such a wretched condition again."

The camp was further cheered by the arrival

After a brutal winter, the soldiers rejoiced when supply wagons arrived at Valley Forge in the spring.

Martha Washington visits the troops at Valley Forge.

of George Washington's wife, Martha. Lady Washington, as she was called, journeyed to Valley Forge in February. She was a strong woman with a warm smile, and her presence gave comfort to the weary and sick men.

Spring finally came to Valley Forge. To the suffering men, the gradually warmer days seemed a miracle. An even more astonishing miracle occurred in the Schuylkill River, which wound through the camp. With the breakup of the ice, the river suddenly became alive with fish. Spring warmth brought whole schools of shad swarming through the stream. It seemed to the hungry Americans that the fish were a gift

20

from God. Armed with baskets, pitchforks, and even tree branches, Washington's soldiers plunged into the chilly waters to scoop out the wriggling fish. The men happily feasted on fresh fish for weeks.

The greatest boost to the morale of Washington's men came from Europe. Since the war's beginning, European intellectuals and idealists had looked upon the American Revolution as a great crusade. In the American wilderness, a colonial people were attempting to establish a bold new society. The society intended to reject the Old World practice of kings, queens, and powerful landlords ruling the masses.

Kazimierz Pulaski

Most of the European idealists who came to America were themselves Old World aristocrats. Nevertheless, they entertained the radical belief that a person should be judged by his character instead of by the family into which he had been born. Many were experienced army officers who hoped to teach Americans how to fight against European professional soldiers. From Poland came Pulaski and Kosciuszko. From France came the young Marquis de Lafayette, who grew to idolize George Washington. And from Prussia came an old warhorse of a soldier, the Baron Friedrich von Steuben.

Tadeusz Kosciuszko

Baron von Steuben had served as an officer under the brilliant Prussian leader Frederick the Great. Although his military career had ended

long before he came to America, von Steuben
was skilled at teaching precision marching to
infantrymen. The ability to drill was essential
when fighting the British, whose ranks of men
marched into battle as smartly as if they were
on a parade field. When the Baron reported to
Valley Forge, Washington took an instant liking
to him. Von Steuben gasped, however, when
he first observed the marching abilities of
Washington's soldiers. They were disorganized
and untrained in basic marching techniques.

Starting with a small group, von Steuben
taught the men basics—the proper way to stand
at attention, left face, right face, forward march,
flank march. The job was difficult and time-

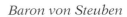

consuming. One witness wrote that the former Prussian officer grew so frustrated with the amateur soldiers' many mistakes that he began to "swear in German, then in French, and then in both languages together." Finally he pleaded for someone to "swear for me in English."

Still, the Baron drilled the men on the muddy fields from sunup to sundown. When he was satisfied that his first small group knew how to march, he sent them back to their units to teach their comrades. The Baron then began teaching another group himself.

A Revolution-era cannon

Baron von Steuben was a strict drillmaster, but he was constantly fascinated by the unique American troops he was instructing. He quickly learned that he had to treat the free-spirited Americans differently from the quick-to-obey Prussians. In Prussia "you say to your soldier, 'Do this' and he does it," wrote von Steuben. "But [here] I am obliged to say, 'This is the reason why you ought to do that,' and then he does it."

A new army emerged from Valley Forge in the summer of 1778. It bore little resemblance to the wretched band of troops that had limped into the camp six months earlier. Thanks to the quartermaster, Nathanael Greene, the army was better equipped. Thanks to the influence of von Steuben and the other Europeans, both the officers and the men were more professional.

Washington and von Steuben at Valley Forge— in a matter of months, the German general had turned Washington's army into a well-trained fighting machine.

Moreover, everyone from private to colonel felt that their dreadful winter experience at Valley Forge had made them better soldiers. They marched out of the camp convinced that if they had endured that terrible winter, they surely could take anything the British could give them.

Finally, none of the men would ever forget that their general, George Washington, had suffered through the miserable winter at their side. After a succession of depressing defeats, many soldiers had begun to doubt the leadership ability of their commanding officer. But seeing Washington sharing their hardships at Valley Forge day after day convinced the men that they could follow this commander to the end of the war.

Washington's leadership ability shone during the Battle of Monmouth, the army's first encounter after Valley Forge. During the vicious fighting, a large American unit began to retreat. Washington met the fleeing Americans, and according to the Marquis de Lafayette, his "presence stopped the retreat . . . his calm courage gave him the air best calculated to excite enthusiasm." Lafayette told how Washington galloped his horse "all along the lines amid the shouts of the soldiers, cheering them by his voice and example, and restoring to our standard the fortunes of the

fight. I thought then, as now, that never had I beheld so superb a man."

At the Battle of Monmouth, the British realized they were no longer fighting against the ragtag soldiers they had faced in 1777. The British were shocked to see that the amateur Americans had suddenly become professionals commanded by an outstanding leader. For Washington's men, the bitter lessons of Valley Forge had reaped a great reward.

The rejuvenated Americans swarm over the British at Monmouth.

Today, Valley Forge, Pennsylvania, is a sprawling park that covers more than 3,000 acres. The original stone house that served as Washington's headquarters still stands there. Rows of log huts have been carefully reconstructed as replicas of the ones that once housed eleven thousand half-starved men. The park serves as a memorial honoring those courageous men who stood with George Washington during their country's darkest hour.

Modern reconstructions at Valley Forge show visitors the soldiers' log huts (above left; left) and George Washington's desk (above right). Re-creations of battle drills are also staged for visitors to the park (below).

After the winter of 1777–78, the American army marched forward to victory and eventually won independence for their nation. But the period of peril that was climaxed by the painful winter at Valley Forge will always be remembered in the words of Thomas Paine:

The summer soldier and the sunshine patriot, will, in this crisis, shrink from the service of his country; but he that stands it now, deserves the love and thanks of man and woman. Tyranny, like hell, is not easily conquered; yet we have this consolation with us, that the harder the conflict the more glorious the triumph.

The United States Memorial Arch was constructed in 1917 as a monument to all those who served at Valley Forge.

INDEX

PHOTO CREDITS

Cover, Stock Montage; 1, *March to Valley Forge,* painted by William B. Trego/Courtesy The Valley Forge Historical Society; 2, *Before the Dawn,* painted by ©J.L.G. Ferris/Archives of '76, Bay Village, Ohio; 3, 4, 5, 6, 7, North Wind Picture Archives; 8–9, *The Camp of the American Army at Valley Forge 1778,* painted by Edwin Austin Abbey/Courtesy The Commonwealth of Pennsylvania, Capitol Preservation Committee, photograph ©Brian Hunt; 10, 11, 12, North Wind; 13, Courtesy The Valley Forge National Historical Park; 14, 15 (both photos), 16, 18, North Wind; 19, Bettmann Archive; 20, 21 (both pictures), North Wind; 22, Bettmann Archive; 23, 24, North Wind; 25, Stock Montage Inc.; 27 (both pictures), Bettmann Archive; 28, ©John Ansley; 29 (top left and top right), North Wind; 29 (center and bottom), 30, Courtesy The Valley Forge National Historical Park; 31, ©John Ansley

Picture Identifications:
page 1: Washington and his troops struggle through their march to Valley Forge.
page 2: George Washington is consoled by wife Martha.

Project Editors: Shari Joffe and Mark Friedman
Design and Electronic Composition: TJS Design
Photo Editor: Jan Izzo
Cornerstones of Freedom Logo: David Cunningham

ABOUT THE AUTHOR

R. Conrad Stein was born and grew up in Chicago. He graduated from the University of Illinois with a degree in history, and he later studied in Mexico. He is the author of more than eighty published books for young readers.

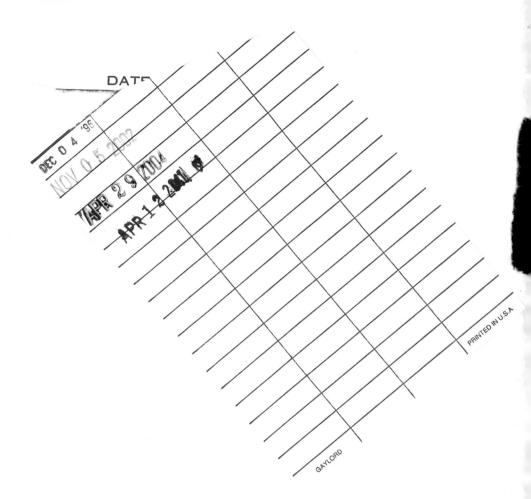

DATE

DEC 0 4 '96

NOV 0 5 2002

APR 2 9 2004

APR 1 2 2004

PRINTED IN U.S.A.

GAYLORD